SUPERSTARS
of
PRO FOOTBALL

TONY GONZALEZ

Amy Hunter

Mason Crest Publishers

Produced by OTTN Publishing in association with
21st Century Publishing and Communications, Inc.

MASON CREST PUBLISHERS INC.
370 Reed Road
Broomall, Pennsylvania 19008
(866) MCP-BOOK (toll free)
www.masoncrest.com

Printed in the United States of America.

First Printing

9 8 7 6 5 4 3 2 1

Library of Congress Cataloging-in-Publication Data

Hunter, Amy N.
   Tony Gonzalez / Amy Hunter.
      p. cm. — (Superstars of pro football)
   Includes bibliographical references.
   ISBN-13: 978-1-4222-0541-9 (hardcover) — ISBN-10: 1-4222-0541-X (hardcover)
   ISBN-13: 978-1-4222-0824-3 (pbk.) — ISBN-10: 1-4222-0824-9 (pbk.)
   1. Gonzalez, Tony, 1976–   —Juvenile literature. 2. Football players—United
States—Biography—Juvenile literature. I. Title.
GV939.G655H86 2008
796.332092—dc22
[B]   2008028192

Publisher's note:
All quotations in this book come from original sources, and contain the spelling
and grammatical inconsistencies of the original text.

◀◀ CROSS-CURRENTS ▶▶

In the ebb and flow of the currents of life we are each influenced
by many people, places, and events that we directly experience or
have learned about. Throughout the chapters of this book you will
come across **CROSS-CURRENTS** reference bubbles. These bubbles
direct you to a **CROSS-CURRENTS** section in the back of the
book that contains fascinating and informative sidebars
and related pictures. Go on. ▶▶

‹‹CONTENTS››

BACK TO THE PRO BOWL

Each year, the best players in the National Football League (NFL) are invited to play in an all-star game held a week after the Super Bowl. In December 2007, Kansas City's Tony Gonzalez was chosen to play in the Pro Bowl for the ninth time. This set an NFL record for the most Pro Bowl appearances by a **tight end**.

CROSS-CURRENTS

To learn more about the NFL's annual all-star game, read "A History of the Pro Bowl." Go to page 46. ▶▶

Soon after Tony was chosen to play in the 2008 Pro Bowl, Chiefs president Carl Peterson spoke about Tony's value to his team and to the Kansas City area:

Kansas City Chiefs tight end Tony Gonzalez is one of the best tight ends in NFL history. He holds records for most career catches and touchdowns by a tight end, and has been selected for the Pro Bowl nine times.

"Very few players have demonstrated the outstanding level of consistency that Tony has demonstrated over the years. As both a player and a person, Kansas City is fortunate to have Tony as a member of our community."

Tony had a very strong year in 2007, his 11th season in the NFL. He led all Chiefs' receivers with 99 catches and scored five touchdowns. Tony gained 1,172 yards—an average of 11.8 yards per catch. This was the third time in his career that Tony had gained more than 1,000 receiving yards in a season—something only three other tight ends had ever done in the history of the NFL.

Tony broke two NFL records during the 2007 season. He finished the year with 820 career receptions and 66 career touchdowns. This broke records that had been set by Shannon Sharpe, a great tight end who had played 14 seasons with the Denver Broncos and Baltimore

Tony Gonzalez of the Kansas City Chiefs celebrates after catching his 63rd career touchdown pass, October 14, 2007. That catch set a new record for most career touchdowns scored by a tight end.

Ravens. (Sharpe had caught 815 passes, including 62 touchdowns, during his career.) At the end of the 2007 season, Tony was poised to break another NFL record for tight ends. His 9,882 career receiving yards were second in NFL history to Sharpe's 10,060 receiving yards.

Tony has spoken about what it means to him to pass other great tight ends in the NFL's record book:

> **"It means a lot. . . . I do take satisfaction in [breaking records], especially considering guys like tight end Shannon Sharpe [had] the record[s]. . . . [Setting records is] something that I definitely have to take satisfaction on since [I've] worked so hard to get there. It's also one of those things that I don't want to define who I am. I still have to keep going out there. I want to score touchdowns, not because I'm trying to set a record, but because I think our team needs it."**

The 2008 Pro Bowl

Tony was joined in the 2008 Pro Bowl by teammate Jared Allen, a defensive end who made his first appearance in the all-star game. The two traveled to Hawaii's Aloha Stadium, where the Pro Bowl is played each year. Tony and his teammate were on the American Football Conference (AFC) team. They would play against a team of the best players from the NFL's National Football Conference (NFC).

CROSS-CURRENTS

Read "Multiple Pro Bowl Appearances" to learn more about the players who have been selected to the most Pro Bowls. Go to page 47. ▶▶

When the game began, the AFC team got off to an early lead. Tony had a big part in the team's success. In the first quarter, AFC quarterback Peyton Manning hit Tony with a 29-yard pass. Soon after this, Tony grabbed another long pass, this one for 25 yards. This moved the AFC team to the NFC's 32-yard-line. After another long pass, San Diego fullback Lorenzo Neal scored a one-yard touchdown. This gave the AFC a 7–0 lead.

At one point early in the second quarter, the AFC team held a 24–7 lead. However, the NFC squad mounted a comeback. Early in the third quarter, the NFC scored to take the lead, 28–27. After this, Tony helped his team score again. Tony started a third-quarter drive

Tony attempts to break away after a catch during the 2008 Pro Bowl. Although he caught four passes for 79 yards during the all-star game, Tony's AFC team lost to the NFC squad.

with an 11-yard reception that moved the AFC team near the 50-yard line. After several penalties moved the team into NFC territory, AFC kicker Rob Bironas of the Tennessee Titans booted a 28-yard field goal. This put the AFC team back in the lead, 30–28.

The NFC team pulled away with two scores in the final quarter, however, and won the 2008 Pro Bowl, 42–30. Tony caught a pass for 14 yards and a first down during one fourth-quarter drive, but after his catch the AFC's drive stalled. Overall, though, it had been a productive game for Tony. He finished with four catches, and his 79 yards led all AFC receivers.

A Hero on and off the Field

Tony Gonzalez is one of the best tight ends ever to play in the NFL. His many trips to the Pro Bowl, and the many records he has set, are proof of his talent. When Tony's career ends, it is likely that he will be elected to the Pro Football Hall of Fame.

Despite Tony's great natural ability, his success has not been an accident. Tony has spent his career refining his game. He has experimented with his diet, fitness routines, and game strategies in order to be the best.

Tony Gonzalez is a hero off the field as well as on it. He has established a charitable foundation to help sick children. He helps disadvantaged young people by working with the Boys and Girls Clubs of America. He served as a celebrity judge on the television program *Oprah's Big Give*, which worked to raise money for various charities. And in July 2008, while eating dinner in a restaurant in California, Tony performed the **Heimlich maneuver** on a man who was choking. Afterward, the choking man, Ken Hunter, said that Tony's quick reaction kept him from dying:

> **"Tony saved my life. There's no doubt. . . . Thank God he was there."**

Whether he is helping other people, or helping his team score touchdowns, Tony Gonzalez has become one of the most admired NFL stars today.

A
Gifted Athlete

Tony Gonzalez was born on February 27, 1976, in Torrance, California, a suburb of Los Angeles. His mother, Judy Gonzalez, worked two jobs to support Tony and his older brother, Chris. When Tony was growing up, he liked to ride his bike and his skateboard. He also enjoyed spending time with his friends.

Chris Gonzalez was a good athlete, and he encouraged Tony to play sports. When Tony was 11, he tried out for a Pop Warner football team in Huntington Beach, California. He hated it and quit the team. The next year, Tony rejoined the team. This time, he stuck it out—even though his coaches only allowed him on the field for six plays in each game. Tony later said,

"I was awful at football when I was a little kid. I didn't have the aggressiveness. I was just a nice kid. I didn't want to hurt anyone. I played Pop Warner because my older brother, Chris, did. I was big, but I was just a puddin'—everybody pushed me around.**"**

When he was in eighth grade, Tony had trouble with some older bullies. He would race home from school each afternoon, trying to

When Tony Gonzalez was born, his family lived in Torrance, California (pictured above), a city of about 140,000 residents near Los Angeles. Tony's family eventually moved to the nearby city of Huntington Beach.

avoid them. At his eighth-grade graduation, Tony hurried off the stage so that he could hide from the bullies. Tony said that he felt pitiful when his family saw him running away at the ceremony:

"It embarrassed me because I was a wimp. . . . I went to hide behind a wall, and my family saw me there. My mom didn't say a word. She just gave me this look like she was disappointed. I promised myself I would never run from anything again."

The next time Tony saw the bullies, he was able to face them without running away. This helped his confidence. So did learning that he had the size and skill to play basketball. During the summer after eighth grade Tony joined a basketball league. He scored 18 points in his first game. Success helped Tony come out of his shell. He even decided to give football another try. Tony explained:

"The next year, I went out for football at the high school because my brother was playing. The first day of practice, Eric Escobedo, a friend of mine, looked up and said, 'Gonzalez? What are you doing back out there?' Well, he didn't know I was different. After basketball, well, I got it. I figured it out. I could play football too."

Football Success

Tony learned quickly. By the fall of 1993, his senior year at Huntington Beach High School, he was one of the best players in the state. That year he caught 62 passes for 945 yards, and scored 13 touchdowns. He also played linebacker on defense. At the end of the season, he was named an All-American.

During high school, Tony also won varsity letters in baseball and basketball. During his senior year, he averaged 26 points a game and broke the school's scoring record. As a result, Tony shared the 1994 Orange County High School Athlete of the Year Award with another great athlete, golfer Tiger Woods.

CROSS-CURRENTS

Read "Sharing the Fame" to learn more about Tony's chief competitor for the 1994 Orange County Athlete of the Year Award. Go to page 48. ▶▶

Tony had a tough childhood. His father was rarely around, and when Tony was in middle school he experienced trouble with older bullies. Success at sports—particularly basketball—helped to build Tony's confidence.

Tony's athletic success drew attention from college coaches. At one point, he was receiving 30 to 40 **scholarship** offers a week. Tony eventually decided to attend the University of California at Berkeley. Tony would be able to play both football and basketball at Berkeley, and he would still be close to home.

College Years

At Berkeley, Tony studied communications and also took some acting classes. Out of the classroom, he focused on sports. In 1994, his first season on Berkeley's football team, Tony caught eight passes, including one for a touchdown. But the Golden Bears struggled, finishing with a 4–7 record.

Tony continued to improve as a football player during his sophomore year. Although Berkeley won just three of 11 games,

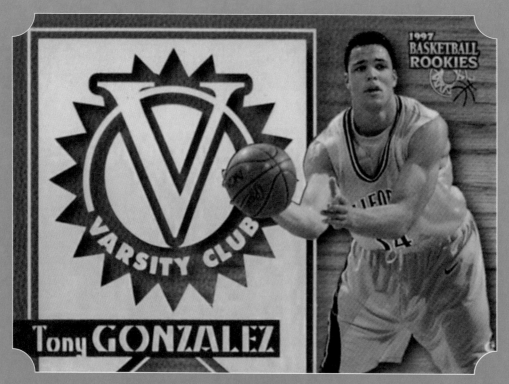

This trading card shows Tony in action with California's basketball team. For most of his three seasons with the Golden Bears, Tony was a bench player. He was a solid scorer and rebounder.

Tony put up good numbers. He caught 37 passes for 541 yards and two touchdowns.

Tony continued to play basketball during his time at Berkley. As a freshman, he averaged more than seven points and nearly four rebounds a game. In his sophomore season, 1995–96, Tony scored 5.3 points per game and helped the Golden Bears to a 17–11 record. That was good enough for an invitation to the NCAA Tournament.

Before Tony's junior year, Berkeley hired a new football coach. Steve Mariucci had coached with the NFL's Green Bay Packers. He wanted to implement the NFL's **West Coast offense** at Berkeley. Tony benefited from the pro-style offense. In his junior season, he caught 46 passes for 699 yards and scored five touchdowns. He gained more receiving yards than any other tight end in the country. This performance earned Tony a spot on both the All–Pac-10 Conference team and the All-American team.

Leaving School

In 1996–97, Tony had another solid basketball season. He averaged 6.8 points and 4.5 rebounds per game. The Golden Bears finished with a 23–9 record and reached the NCAA Tournament again. One of Tony's best games came in the second round of the tournament, when he scored 23 points against Villanova. The Golden Bears reached the Sweet 16, where they were eliminated by one of the country's top teams, North Carolina.

When the basketball season ended, Tony decided that he was ready to pursue a career in professional football. He announced that he would make himself eligible for the 1997 NFL **draft**.

CROSS-CURRENTS

To learn more about Tony's strong performances in the 1997 NCAA Tournament, read "Headed to the Sweet 16." Go to page 49. ▶▶

A RISING STAR

In 1996, the Kansas City Chiefs had one of the least productive offenses in the National Football League. The team's head coach, Marty Schottenheimer, hoped to improve the Chiefs' offense by drafting talented young players. The coach thought Tony Gonzalez could help the team score more points. Schottenheimer began planning to bring Tony to Kansas City.

Going into the 1997 NFL draft, the Chiefs had the 18th overall pick. Tony's pass-catching skills had impressed many teams, however, so the tight end was expected to be among the first 15 players chosen. To make sure that Kansas City had a shot at Tony, Schottenheimer made a deal with the Houston Oilers.

A trading card from Tony's first season with the Chiefs. After being chosen with the 13th pick in the 1997 NFL draft, Tony made the team as a backup tight end.

Kansas City traded four draft picks to Houston. In exchange, the Oilers gave the Chiefs their first-round pick, the 13th overall. The Chiefs used this pick to select Tony.

First Season With the Chiefs

Rookie players—even first-round draft picks—often do not make much of an impact in their first NFL season. Players need time to adjust to the speed of the professional game. Tony made the team as a backup tight end, but the coaches knew he still had a lot to learn. His playing time would be limited. This would give Tony a chance to watch veteran players while developing his own skills.

The Chiefs were a much better team in 1997 than they had been the previous season. The offense scored 375 points, the fifth-best total

A huge crowd cheers the Chiefs as they run onto the field at Arrowhead Stadium during a game. The stadium, which seats more than 79,000 fans, is considered one of the loudest in the NFL.

in the NFL. (In 1996, the Chiefs' offense had been ranked 24th among the league's 30 teams.) Kansas City finished with a 13–3 record and earned a playoff spot.

Tony came off the bench to catch 33 passes for 368 yards, an average of 11.2 yards per catch. He scored his first NFL touchdown on October 5, 1997, catching a 21-yard pass in a game against the Miami Dolphins. In a November game against the Jacksonville Jaguars, he caught a season-high seven passes. His second touchdown catch of the season came three weeks later, in a win over the San Francisco 49ers.

In his first playoff game, Tony had three receptions, including a 12-yard pass for a touchdown. However, the Denver Broncos pulled out a 14–10 win, ending Kansas City's season. Denver would go on to win the Super Bowl, while Tony and the Chiefs watched from home.

Learning Curve

Tony's first NFL season had been solid, but it was not without problems. He had dropped passes and missed tackles. Although Tony was strong and fast, he still had to learn how to play the tight end position. Kansas City's coaches were patient, though. They could see Tony's raw talent, and knew that the weaknesses in his game could be corrected through practice and hard work.

CROSS-CURRENTS

Read "The Tight End Position" to learn more about the demands of Tony's job on the football field. Go to page 50. ▶▶

During the off-season, Tony trained hard in the weight room. At the beginning of the 1998 season, he was named the Chiefs' starting tight end. However, he continued to struggle. In the team's first game, he caught three passes but also fumbled twice. After 11 games, he had just 35 catches and no touchdowns. A sportswriter for a local newspaper gave Tony a grade of D-minus for his performance to that point in the season. Tony later explained how he felt:

❝I'd never gotten a D-minus in anything. D-minus? People were stopping me on the street, calling me at home, asking what was the matter. I didn't have an answer. I'd never worked so hard preparing for a season. I'd put in all these hours in the weight room, out on the field, and I had nothing to show for it. I was confused.❞

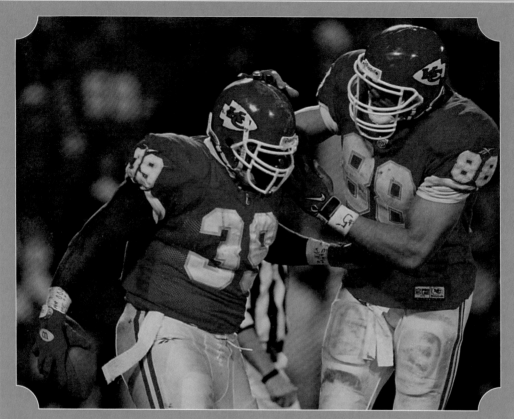

Tony celebrates with teammate Bam Morris (number 39) during a 1998 game against the Dallas Cowboys. In the second half of the 1998 season, Tony began to emerge as a star.

Part of the reason for Tony's struggles was that the Chiefs' coaches had created **complex** plays for the tight end. The coaches decided to simplify the game plan. Tony responded to the changes. In his last five games, he caught 23 passes, including two touchdowns. Chiefs fans could finally see what the 22-year-old was capable of doing on the football field.

Tony's final statistics for the 1998 season were pretty good. He finished with 59 receptions, the second-highest figure on the team. He gained 621 yards and scored twice. However, Kansas City did not play as well in 1998 as it had the previous year. The team had gotten off to a quick start, winning four of its first five games, but then lost five in a row. The Chiefs finished with a 7–9 record. At the end of the disappointing season, Marty Schottenheimer resigned as the team's head coach.

Charitable Work

Tony recognized that as a professional athlete, fans would watch his actions both on and off the field. In 1998, he established the Tony Gonzalez Foundation. Tony's goal for this charitable organization was to help people who are less fortunate. The foundation provides supports to several organizations, including the Boys and Girls Clubs of America and the Shadow Buddies program.

 The Tony Gonzalez Foundation

tonygonzalezfoundation.shadowbuddies.org

Foundation Goals

Supports the Shadow Buddies Foundation and the Boys and Girls Club of America

Shadow Buddies

Boys & Girls Club of America

Kansas City Chiefs Page

NFL Home Page

Sponsorship Info

* The purpose of the Tony Gonzalez Foundation is to serve as a positive force in the lives of individuals in need, no matter their age, financial status, ethnic background, physical abilities or limitations.

My foundation focuses on assisting with emotional and educational support by helping medically challenged children through the Shadow Buddies Foundation, and providing support for the disadvantaged youth through The Boys and Girls Club.

Since entering the NFL, Tony has spent his spare time trying to help others. The Web site of his charitable foundation (http://tonygonzalezfoundation.shadowbuddies.org) provides information about the many worthwhile organizations that Tony helps to support.

The Boys and Girls Clubs of America provide a place for children to play and learn after school and on the weekends. The Shadow Buddies program provides children who are experiencing a medical crisis with a doll. The dolls are made to look like each child and to represent the child's medical condition. They are meant to provide comfort to the children while they are in a hospital undergoing scary medical tests or painful procedures. The Shadow Buddies program also provides Senior Buddies to older people in long-term care facilities or hospitals.

CROSS-CURRENTS

To learn more about a charitable group that Tony supports, read "The Boys and Girls Clubs of America." Go to page 50. ▶▶

As part of his work with Shadow Buddies, Tony's foundation has distributed "Know Your Buddy" kits to schools around the country. These kits encourage children to be kind and understanding when they meet young people who are suffering from a medical condition.

Tony also donates his time and money to other organizations. He has said that volunteering and helping the communities where he lives and works are important:

> **[W]hen you look back on your career and what you've done, sure, [people are] going to look at what you did on the football field, but I think people respect what you did off the field, especially when you can touch people's lives.**

Coming into His Own

Before the 1999 season, Gunther Cunningham, the Chiefs' former **defensive coordinator**, was hired as the new head coach. Tony missed the first game of the 1999 season, but when he returned to the starting lineup, he was ready to play. In Kansas City's third game, Tony caught seven passes, including a 15-yard touchdown, in a win over Detroit. He scored two touchdowns in a 35–8 win over the Baltimore Ravens, and caught eight passes in a November game against the Seattle Seahawks. In an exciting 37–34 win over the Oakland Raiders, Tony caught a pass and ran 73 yards for a touchdown. A few weeks later, in a game against the Pittsburgh Steelers, Tony caught six passes for 93 yards and two more scores.

Tony was modest when he tried to explain his success. After the Pittsburgh game, he explained to *Sports Illustrated* that he had needed time to adjust to the NFL:

> **"The third year is when everything finally clicks in for me. I'm not sure why that is. High school? I was nothing until my junior year. College? The same thing. I was an All-American as a junior. The NFL? Here it is all over again."**

By the end of the 1999 season, Tony was considered one of the best tight ends in the NFL. He set team records for most catches (76)

Tony celebrates after scoring his second touchdown in the Chiefs' 35–19 victory over Pittsburgh, December 18, 1999. By the end of the 1999 season, many people considered Tony the best tight end in the NFL.

and touchdowns (11) in a season by a tight end. His strong season helped the Chiefs finish the season with a winning record. However, Kansas City's nine victories were not enough for a playoff spot.

After the season, Tony was rewarded with an invitation to play in the Pro Bowl for the first time. He caught four passes—one for a touchdown—and helped the AFC team win, 51–31.

Personal Success, Team Frustration

In 2000, Tony had an even more productive season. He had 93 receptions for 1,203 yards and scored nine touchdowns. Six times, Tony gained more than 100 yards receiving in a game. On December 4, against the New England Patriots, Tony caught 11 passes for 147 yards. He was named to the Pro Bowl for the second time. Unfortunately, the Chiefs had another **lackluster** season. The team finished 7–9 and missed the playoffs again.

After the season, Kansas City's management made changes. Cunningham was fired as the head coach. Dick Vermeil, a respected coach who had led the St. Louis Rams to a Super Bowl victory in January 2000, was hired to coach the Chiefs in 2001. The Chiefs also brought in several new players to help improve the offense. Priest Holmes joined the team as a running back, while Trent Green took over as the team's quarterback.

Off the field, Tony experienced changes in his personal life as well. On February 21, 2001, Tony became a father when his girlfriend, Lauren Sánchez, gave birth to a baby boy, Nikko Gonzalez. At the time Sánchez was a television news reporter in Los Angeles. Although Tony and Lauren eventually broke up, he has tried to be a responsible father to Nikko.

Hard Times in Kansas City

Despite all of the changes, the Chiefs struggled in 2001. The team finished with a 6–10 record. Tony's season was solid, though not as spectacular as 2000. Tony finished the 2001 season with 73 catches for 917 yards and six touchdowns. He made the Pro Bowl squad again, but did not play in the game because of a knee injury.

Although the season was disappointing, off the field Tony had some notable accomplishments. The Boys and Girls Club of Greater Kansas City gave Tony its Role Model of the Year Award. One thing

Quarterback Trent Green (number 10) threw 24 interceptions in 2001, his first season with the Chiefs. Green's problems affected the entire team, and Kansas City finished the 2001 season with a losing record.

that made the award particularly meaningful to Tony was that children who attended the area's Boys and Girls Clubs voted to honor him.

Also in 2001, Tony took over the Chiefs' "Shop With a Jock" program. Shop With a Jock gathers foster children from the Kansas City area and treats them to dinner and a trip to a local department store for Christmas shopping. Linebacker Donnie Edwards had developed the program. When Edwards left the Chiefs, Tony stepped in to continue the charitable work.

THE RECORD BREAKER

The 2001 season had not gone the way that Chiefs' fans had hoped. At the end of the season, the Chiefs had to deal with a new problem. The contract that Tony Gonzalez had signed before his rookie season was about to expire. Now that he had emerged as an NFL star, Tony expected a big pay raise.

In the summer of 2002 the Chiefs offered Tony a new contract. The deal would have made Tony the highest-paid tight end in NFL history. It included a bonus of $8 million just for signing the contract. However, there was one condition. To get the deal, Tony would have to give up his dream of playing professional basketball. Tony had continued playing the sport

When Kansas City offered Tony a new contract before the 2002 season, the team asked him to stop playing basketball. The team was afraid that if Tony got hurt, he would not be able to play football anymore.

CROSS-CURRENTS

When he's not playing football, Tony is involved with many projects. To learn about one of them, read "Catch and Connect." Go to page 52. ▶▶

during the off-season. He had even played with the Miami Heat's summer-league team, until suffering an ankle injury.

Tony refused the offer. Although Kansas City had offered a large amount of money, Tony believed that he should be paid like a top wide receiver. (Typically, wide receivers earn much more than tight ends). Tony threatened to sit out for the entire 2002 season if the Chiefs did not give him a contract he felt was fair.

In response, the Chiefs named Tony a **franchise player**. Under NFL rules, this meant that the team could offer Tony a one-year contract. His salary would be based on the average of the previous year's top five salaries for tight ends. In Tony's case, the salary would be about $3 million a year—much lower than he had originally been offered.

NFL players don't want a one-year contract because football players are at a high risk for injuries. If a player on a one-year contract gets hurt during that season, the player could lose the chance to negotiate a new contract. Tony was not happy about the franchise tag. At first, he refused to report to training camp. Eventually, though, Tony signed the one-year deal. He rejoined the team just in time for the start of the 2002 season.

The 2002 Season

Tony was back in the starting lineup for the first game of 2002. He showed that he was ready to play by catching five passes for 87 yards, including a touchdown. This helped Kansas City beat the Cleveland Browns in an exciting shootout, 40–39.

Less than a week later, Tony and the Chiefs agreed on a seven-year contract worth $31 million. The new deal included a $10 million signing bonus. When the contract was announced, Tony said:

"The best part is knowing I'll be a Chief for life. I don't have to move or do any of that other stuff that goes with moving to a new team. I'm just happy to have this thing done."

Tony justified the big contract with another solid year in 2002. He finished with 63 receptions for 773 yards and seven touchdowns. One of his best performances came in the season's fourth game. Against the Miami Dolphins, he caught seven passes for 140 yards. He scored three touchdowns, including one on a 42-yard run.

However, the Chiefs were never able to put together a long winning streak in 2002. Kansas City ended the season with eight wins and eight losses, and missed the playoffs once gain.

After the 2002 season, Tony was chosen to go to the Pro Bowl for the fourth time. He put on a good performance in the all-star game, catching five passes for 98 yards and a touchdown as the AFC won easily, 45–20.

Tony hangs on to the ball after making a catch in a 2002 game against the Oakland Raiders. The star tight end showed Kansas City fans that he deserved his big contract, catching seven touchdowns in 2002.

Back to the Playoffs

Although the Chiefs had not performed up to expectations, there were promising signs. In 2002 Kansas City's offense had scored more points than any other team in the NFL. Quarterback Trent Green had an excellent second season with the Chiefs, throwing 26 touchdown passes. Running back Priest Holmes had gained 1,615 yards, third best in the NFL, and had scored 21 touchdowns. The team seemed to be going in the right direction. All the pieces were in place for Kansas City to make a playoff run.

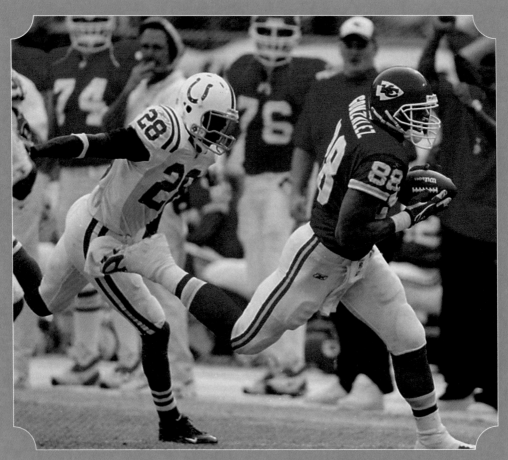

Tony heads upfield after catching a pass during Kansas City's playoff game against the Colts, January 11, 2004. Tony caught passes of 16, 22, 8, and 9 yards. Another catch—a 27-yard touchdown—was wiped out because of a penalty.

The Chiefs jumped out to a great start, winning their first nine games of 2003. It was the best start to a season in the team's history. Tony was a major part of the team's success, but he was not the only contributor. During the season Priest Holmes set a new NFL record for most rushing touchdowns in a season, with 27. Dante Hall returned four kicks for touchdowns. Trent Green threw for more than 4,000 yards. Tony caught 71 of Green's passes, gaining 916 yards and scoring 10 touchdowns. Once again, the Chiefs led the NFL in scoring.

Kansas City finished the 2003 season with a 13–3 record. That was good enough to win the AFC West Division and earn a playoff spot. The game would be played at home against the Indianapolis Colts, a wild-card team. The home-field advantage did not help the Chiefs, however. Although Tony caught four passes for 55 yards, the Colts upset Kansas City, 38–31.

Once again, Tony was named to the AFC's Pro Bowl squad. This time, he was joined by many of his teammates, including Holmes, Green, Hall, fullback Tony Richardson, offensive linemen Willie Roaf and Will Shields, and defensive players Gary Stills and Jerome Woods. The Pro Bowl game was a high-scoring affair. The two teams combined for 107 points, the most ever scored in a Pro Bowl. Tony had five catches for 56 yards. One was a second-quarter touchdown on a nine-yard pass from Peyton Manning—quarterback of the Colts team that had knocked Kansas City out of the playoffs.

A Step Backward

With the success of 2003 behind them, Tony and his teammates expected 2004 to be another good year. However, Kansas City struggled when the season started. The team lost its first three games, and eight of its first 11. Although the Chiefs finished strong, winning four of their last five games, the year ended with Kansas City missing the playoffs once again. The team finished with a 7–9 record.

Individually, 2004 was Tony's finest season. In six games, he surpassed 100 yards receiving, including a 14-catch, 144-yard game against the San Diego Chargers in the season's final contest. Tony's 102 catches led the NFL, and set an NFL record for the most receptions in a season by a tight end. His 1,258 receiving yards were the seventh-highest figure in the league. He scored seven touchdowns, and was named to the Pro Bowl for the sixth time.

One of Tony's best performances of 2004 came in the team's seventh game, against Indianapolis. In the first quarter, Tony scored on a 21-yard pass, enabling the Chiefs to tie the game at 7–7. The Chiefs eventually took the lead in the game. However, with less than six minutes left, the Colts scored a touchdown to pull within three points, 38–35. A few minutes later, though, Tony scored his second touchdown of the game on a 14-yard pass. This nailed down the victory for Kansas City, 45–35. Tony finished with eight catches for 125 yards.

Charitable Work

After the 2004 season ended, Tony kept himself busy with charitable work. The Chiefs have a long history of **philanthropy**, and Tony often worked on community projects with other players on the team. In one project, the Chiefs paid to refurbish nine football fields in the Kansas City area, so that young people would have nice facilities in which to play their games. As a result, in 2005 the Chiefs were awarded a Pop Warner NFL Team of the Year Award, to recognize the team's commitment to youth football programs.

CROSS-CURRENTS

Read "A Good Guy" to learn about an honor Tony received in 2004 because of his charitable work. Go to page 53. ▶▶

On his own, Tony donated 200 flag football uniforms to the Kansas City Boys and Girls Clubs. He also helped that organization get a $75,000 grant from the NFL to build a flag football field in Kansas City's Cleveland Park. Tony helped other good causes as well. He served as a spokesperson for both the United Way and the Susan G. Komen Race for the Cure, an event that raises money for breast cancer research.

In 2004, the *Sporting News* chose Tony as the magazine's number-one NFL "Good Guy." The magazine noted:

"How about this image: a burly football player handing out, of all things, dolls. But Chiefs tight end Tony Gonzalez has brought joy to thousands of sick children in hospitals through his intense participation in the Shadow Buddies program."

Two U.S. Navy officers pose with Tony in Honolulu, Hawaii, before the start of the 2005 Pro Bowl. Tony was chosen to participate in the all-star game because of his record-setting 2004 season.

Tony has been recognized by other publications as well. *Ingram's* magazine, a business magazine in Kansas City, named Tony to its "40 under 40" list. This is an annual ranking of Kansas City–area leaders under the age of 40 who have become successful.

Bouncing Back

When the 2005 season began, Tony expected his team to do better than it had in 2004. After catching four passes in a season-opening 27–7 win over the New York Jets, Tony told *Sports Illustrated* that he was more interested in team success than in personal statistics:

Tony scores a touchdown during a 2005 game. During that season, Tony averaged 11.6 yards per catch. He had many longer receptions, including his two touchdowns, which covered 16 and 25 yards.

"It's not about doing what I did last year when I was able to catch 102 balls and break the record for catches by a tight end in a season. We're playing for the Super Bowl. This is my ninth year—the window of opportunity is closing.**"**

In 2005 Tony did not put up the same kinds of spectacular numbers that he had the previous season. He finished with 78 catches for 905 yards and just two touchdowns. Nonetheless, he was a big part of Kansas City's success. One highlight came on October 16, when Tony started his 100th straight game. The next week, he caught seven passes against the Dolphins, and on October 30 he had seven more catches for 97 yards and a touchdown against San Diego. The Chiefs won their last two games of the 2005 season to finish with a 10–6 record. However, Kansas City missed the playoffs again.

After the 2005 season, the Chiefs nominated Tony for the Walter Payton NFL Man of the Year award. This is an award given by the league each year to a football player who shows a commitment to community service as well as starring on the field.

A SEASONED ATHLETE

After the 2005 season, Dick Vermeil announced that he would retire as Kansas City's head coach. To replace Vermeil, the team hired Herman Edwards, a former NFL cornerback. Edwards had been the head coach of the New York Jets since 2001. To bring him to Kansas City, the Chiefs had to trade the Jets their fourth-round draft pick.

Edwards had been an assistant coach with the Chiefs during the early 1990s, although he was gone before Tony joined the team in 1997. In his five seasons as head coach of the Jets, Edwards had led the team to the playoffs three times. Tony told reporters that he was looking forward to working with the new coach:

❝I've heard so much about him, what type of motivator he is, the way he'll get us ready to go through walls. I think that's what we need. We need a guy like that to come in—he played the game before and had such success in New York.**❞**

Off to a Slow Start

In Kansas City's first game of the season, Tony caught 10 passes for 81 yards, including a fourth-quarter touchdown. However, this effort

Before the 2006 season, Kansas City hired Herman Edwards to replace Dick Vermeil as the Chiefs' head coach. Edwards had compiled a 39–41 record in five seasons with the Jets, leading the team to the playoffs three times.

was not enough. The Chiefs lost to Cincinnati, 23–10. More importantly, the team lost a key member. Quarterback Trent Green was knocked unconscious and had to be carried off the field. Backup Damon Huard finished the game. Afterward, the Chiefs reported that Green would be out for several weeks because of a head injury.

The Chiefs struggled in their second game, a loss at Denver. However, the team's offense finally found itself in the next game. Tony caught five passes from Huard as Kansas City crushed the San Francisco 49ers, 41–0.

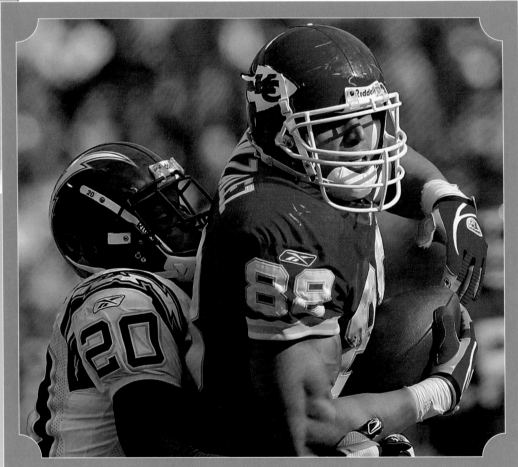

In an October 2006 game against San Diego, Tony made two critical catches during the Chiefs' final drive. This 18-yard grab, in which Tony beat Chargers free safety Marlon McCree, set up a game-winning field goal.

As Huard became more comfortable with the offense, the Chiefs began winning. In the seventh week of the season, the Chiefs found themselves in a 27–27 tie with the San Diego Chargers. With just 33 seconds left in the game, Kansas City got the ball on its own 18-yard line. Huard quickly began moving his team down the field. Tony caught passes for 19 and 18 yards to bring the Chiefs into field-goal range. With 11 seconds left, Chiefs kicker Lawrence Tynes booted a game-winning 53-yard field goal. For Tony, it was a sweet ending to a very good day. He finished as the game's leading receiver, with six catches for 138 yards.

Up-and-Down Season

The victory over the Chargers was the start of a three-game winning streak for the Chiefs. In the third game of that streak, a 31–17 victory over St. Louis, Tony caught a pair of touchdown passes. Later in the season, Tony had another two-touchdown game, this time in a loss to the Browns.

Overall, however, the Chiefs could not win games regularly in 2006. Green finally returned to the starting lineup in mid-November. With Green at quarterback, Kansas City won four of its last seven games to finish with a 9–7 record. Tony was the team's leading receiver, with 73 receptions for 900 yards and five touchdowns. Once again, he was named to the AFC's Pro Bowl team. This time, he was joined by teammates Larry Johnson, Will Shields, and Brian Waters.

CROSS-CURRENTS
Read "A Loss for the Chiefs," to learn about a man who had a great influence on modern pro football. Go to page 54. ▶▶

By winning their last two games, Kansas City earned a wild-card playoff spot. The Chiefs played the Colts in Indianapolis on January 6, 2007. The Colts were prepared, and Kansas City's offense struggled all day. Green connected with Tony on a six-yard touchdown pass, but that was the Chiefs' only touchdown. The Colts won easily, 23–8.

A Busy Off Season

In January 2007, Tony and the Chiefs agreed on a five-year **contract extension**. The deal ensured that Tony would remain the highest-paid tight end in the NFL. Terms were not released to the media, but

Tony was expected to earn at least $17 million with the new contract. When team president Carl Peterson announced the deal, he had high praise for Tony:

> **"Simplistically, we're very pleased to get this done. It will, in all essence, allow Tony Gonzalez to finish his career with the Kansas City Chiefs. The obvious is he's been a very, very productive player for us. I think for our fans in Kansas City it was important for us to get this done. He's done a marvelous job for us both on and off the football field."**

For Tony, the new contract was welcome news. Soon after signing it, however, he experienced some personal health problems. One day, Tony felt a sudden numbness in his face and a sharp pain in his neck. He rushed to the hospital, where doctors examined him. They eventually determined that Tony had developed **Bell's palsy**, a disease that causes the face to become paralyzed temporarily. The disease was treated with medicine. After about a month, the symptoms began to go away.

Although Tony did recover from the illness, it made him worry. He wanted to do whatever he could to be healthy, so that he could continue to play football. In June 2007, Tony tried a new **vegan diet**. He gave up eating meat—including his favorite food, cheeseburgers—and started eating more vegetables, fruits, nuts, and other healthy foods.

CROSS-CURRENTS

To learn more about the special diet that Tony tried in 2007, read "The Vegan Lifestyle." Go to page 55. ▶▶

Before the 2007 season began, Tony organized and directed the Tony Gonzalez Youth Football Camp. This was the third time that Tony had held a camp to help young players learn how to play football. Some of his teammates came to help out at the camp.

One of the biggest events of Tony's off-season occurred on July 20, 2007. On that day, Tony and his girlfriend, October Russell, invited friends and family to a "formal commitment ceremony." It was not a wedding, but they did exchange vows to stay together. When asked why he wanted to have a commitment ceremony, Tony explained:

Kids participate in a training session at the Tony Gonzalez Youth Football Camp, 2007. Before the 2005, 2006, and 2007 seasons, Tony held a camp to teach young players the basics of football.

"We're not signing any papers, but I wanted the world to know that I love her and want to spend my life with her."

Another Rough Season

The Chiefs started slowly in 2007, losing their first two games of the season. Tony helped his team get back on track in the third game. He caught seven passes for 96 yards in a 13–10 victory over the Minnesota Vikings. The Chiefs won their next game as well, beating the Chargers, 30–16. In that game, Tony had five catches, including a 22-yard touchdown.

Tony caught eight passes for 100 yards in the next game, a loss to Jacksonville. He came right back with nine catches, including two

Tony scores his second touchdown—the 64th of his career—in a 27–20 victory over Cincinnati, October 14, 2007. By the end of the season, Tony had established new records for most touchdowns and most catches by a tight end.

touchdowns, in a 27–20 win over Cincinnati. His first score, on a three-yard pass, was the 63rd touchdown of Tony's career. This set a new record for career touchdowns by a tight end, breaking a mark held by Shannon Sharpe. Afterward, Tony told reporters:

> **❝It wasn't the easiest [catch]. I had to go get it. I was like, 'I'm not letting this one get away. I've been waiting a long time for it.'❞**

When the Chiefs won their next game, the team was finally over .500 for the season, at four wins and three losses. However, things went downhill after this. The team's offense struggled to score, and the Chiefs lost their last nine games of the season. Kansas City's 4–12 record was the team's worst finish in almost 30 years.

In the last game of the season, Tony caught a 17-yard pass in the third quarter. This was his 816th career reception, and set a new NFL record for catches by a tight end. Tony caught four more passes in the game—a 13–10 overtime loss to the Jets—to finish with 99 catches for the season and 820 for his career. With 1,172 receiving yards in 2007, Tony became only the fourth tight end in NFL history to surpass 1,000 receiving yards in three different seasons.

After one of the Chiefs' few wins in 2007, Kansas City quarter-back Damon Huard spoke about Tony's importance to the team:

> **❝He truly is the best tight end to have ever played this game. He's just such a great competitor and what makes him so special is his work ethic and his preparation. He practices like it's a game.❞**

At the end of the 2007 season, Tony made another trip to the Pro Bowl. During the game, Tony had four catches for 79 yards, including a 29-yard reception on the second play of the Pro Bowl. However, the AFC team emerged victorious, 42–30.

What the Future Holds

After the disappointing season, the Chiefs entered a period of rebuilding. Kansas City let many veteran players go. Because the team would rely on younger players, the Chiefs were not expected to

Tony is proud of the things he has accomplished during his career in the NFL. However, his goal for every season remains the same: to help the Chiefs win the Super Bowl.

be very good in 2008. Tony was frustrated—after 11 seasons in the NFL, he knew that he probably only had a few more chances left to win a Super Bowl. But he accepted the role of team leader, and spent time working with the younger players during the team's training camp. He explained:

> **"There are going to be some growing pains. There's no doubt about that. But I think by the end of the year we're going to have a really good football team, and we're going to be that much better next year."**

In the spring of 2008, Tony's personal life experienced a major change. His partner, October, gave birth to a daughter. The couple named the infant Malia.

Through his NFL career, Tony Gonzalez has worked hard to improve himself and play at a high level. When Tony does retire, he will hold many of the most important career records for his position. He may well be voted into the Pro Football Hall of Fame one day. But whatever the future holds, Tony has spoken about how he would like to be remembered:

> **"If they crown me the best [tight end of all time], that's fine. . . . I know sooner or later somebody's going to come along, just like I came along. It's just how it goes. More importantly, I want to make sure I [played the game] the right way, with class on and off the field. That's what's really important to me. You can do it, and you can have a good time."**

A History of the Pro Bowl

The idea to gather the best professional football players at the end of the season for an all-star game first emerged during the 1938 season. In January 1939, an all-star game was held between the NFL champion New York Giants and a team of the best players from other NFL teams. All-star games like this were held for the next three years, until the league eliminated the game in 1943.

The idea of an annual all-star game was revived in 1951. In 1970, when the American Football League (AFL) merged with the National Football League, the game was named the Pro Bowl. Each of the NFL's two conferences—the American Football Conference (AFC) and National Football Conference (NFC)—send a team to the game.

The Pro Bowl is played every year in February, one week after the Super Bowl. Since 1980, the Pro Bowl has been held at Aloha Stadium in Honolulu, Hawaii. This ensures a warm climate and an enjoyable experience for the fans as well as the players and their families. NFL players consider it an honor to be chosen to play in the Pro Bowl.

Until 1995, Pro Bowl participants were chosen by a vote of NFL players and coaches. Since that time, fans have been given the chance to help select players. The votes of the fans, players, and coaches determine who will represent the AFC and NFC in the game. All voters are expected to choose the players who have enjoyed the best seasons.

The Pro Bowl does not feature the rough play of a regular-season game. It is generally more fun than competitive. The players want to win, but they don't want to get hurt or to injure others. The intensity of the game typically does not pick up until the fourth quarter, when the game's outcome hangs in the balance.

The game often features wide-open offenses and a great deal of passing. This makes the Pro Bowl fun to watch, both for fans in the stadium and for the people watching at home on television. The teams usually score many touchdowns. Since 2000, the winning Pro Bowl team has tallied 31 points or more in eight of the nine games. Neither the NFC nor the AFC has been able to dominate the Pro Bowl for a long period of time. Since 1981, neither team has ever won more than three Pro Bowls in a row.

(Go back to page 4.)

Multiple Pro Bowl Appearances

Tony's nine Pro Bowl appearances are a great accomplishment. However, some other players have made even more appearances in the NFL's all-star game. Merlin Olsen, a defensive tackle for the Rams during the 1960s and 1970s, was chosen for the Pro Bowl 14 times. Bruce Matthews, an offensive lineman who played for the Houston Oilers and Tennessee Titans between 1983 and 2001, tied this record. Reggie White, a dominant defensive lineman who played from 1985 to 2000, was selected to the Pro Bowl 13 times. Another defensive player, linebacker Junior Seau, was chosen for the all-star game 12 times during his career.

The Kansas City Chiefs' player with the most Pro Bowl appearances is Will Shields. He played 14 seasons, appearing in the Pro Bowl 12 times before retiring in 2006. Tony, who played most of his career with Shields, is currently tied for second in team history with Bobby Bell, a Chiefs linebacker during the 1960s and 1970s. Both have appeared in nine Pro Bowls. Other players who appeared in the Pro Bowl numerous times while with the Chiefs include defensive tackle Buck Buchanan (eight) and quarterback Len Dawson (six).

(Go back to page 7.) ◀◀

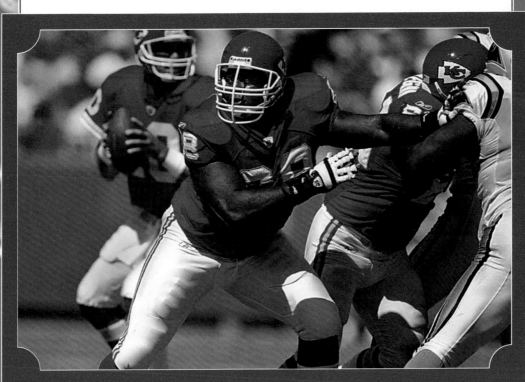

Offensive guard Will Shields (number 68) played his entire 14-season career with Kansas City. He was selected for the Pro Bowl 12 times, and in 2003 received the NFL's Walter Payton Man of the Year Award for his charitable work.

Sharing the Fame

Those who saw Tony Gonzalez play football and basketball in high school knew that they were watching a gifted athlete. Few high school athletes could match Tony's strength, speed, and skills. In any other year, Tony would have been an easy choice for the Athlete of the Year award in his home county. His All-American performance on the football field, and his high-scoring presence on the basketball court, should have ensured that Tony would win the award.

However, during Tony's senior year (1993–94) another athlete from Orange County was receiving national attention. Golfer Eldrick "Tiger" Woods was a senior at Western High School.

He had already won the U.S. Junior Amateur Golf Championship three times, and in 1994 he became the youngest golfer to win the U.S. Amateur Championship. Tiger was so good, he was even invited to play in PGA Tour events. In 1994, Tony and Tiger shared the Orange County Athlete of the Year Award.

Like Tony, Tiger would go on to great success as a professional athlete. Since joining the PGA Tour in 1996, Tiger has won 65 tournaments and over $82 million in prize money. He is widely considered one of the greatest golfers of all time.

(Go back to page 12.)

NFL DRAFT PREDICTIONS | **THE FIRST 32 PICKS**

Sports Illustrated

Tiger WALK

BY RICK REILLY

The Indomitable Tiger Woods Strolled to His Third Masters Title

Playoff Previews

NHL
Red Wings: Unbeatable?

NBA
Lakers: Beatable?

On the 18th at Aug...

Golf great Tiger Woods is featured on a Sports Illustrated cover. Since turning pro in 1996, Tiger has won golf's major tournaments 14 times, a figure that is second only to the legendary Jack Nicklaus (18) in golf history.

Headed to the Sweet 16

One of Tony's most exciting sports moments at the University of California at Berkeley came during his junior year, when the Golden Bears advanced to the Sweet 16 round in the NCAA Men's Basketball Tournament.

When the 1996–97 basketball season began, no one was sure how good California's team would be. In September, a few months before the season started, the team's coach, Todd Bozeman, suddenly quit. The Golden Bears had to quickly hire a new coach, Ben Braun. Also, the team's best player from the previous season, Shareef Abdur-Rahim, had left college early to enter the NBA. Despite the preseason uncertainty, California finished the regular season with a 21–8 record. That was good enough to earn a fifth seeding in the NCAA Tournament's East regional.

In the first round of the tournament, California faced 12th-seeded Princeton. The Tigers were tough—they had won 24 games and lost only three during the regular season. Some people thought Princeton could upset the Golden Bears—after all, in the previous year's NCAA Tournament, the 13th-seeded Tigers had knocked off fourth-seeded UCLA. Also, California's leading scorer, Ed Gray, was out with a broken foot. Tony Gonzalez took Gray's spot in the starting lineup.

The game was close throughout, but in the final minute Tony came up big to help his team win. With just 58 seconds left, and the score tied at 50, Tony hit a jump shot from the baseline to put the Bears ahead. Then, with 33 seconds left, Tony was fouled by a Princeton player. He made one of his two foul shots to give the Bears a 53–50 lead. After Princeton scored to cut California's lead to one point, Tony was fouled again with 15 seconds left. He coolly sank both free throws, sealing a 55–52 victory.

Tony finished the game against Princeton with 13 points. He would do even better in the next round. This time, California's opponent was Villanova, the fourth seed in the East. Tony exploded for a season-high 23 points, leading the Bears to a 75–68 victory.

The Golden Bears faced an even tougher test in its Sweet 16 game. The team's opponent was the East's top-ranked team, North Carolina. California played well but could not handle the Tar Heels, losing the game by a score of 63 to 57. North Carolina went on to defeat Louisville in the Elite Eight, before falling to Arizona, the eventual national champions, in the Final Four.

(Go back to page 15.)

The Tight End Position

Tight end is a position at the end of a football team's offensive line. Also on the offensive line are the center, two guards, and two tackles. The guards line up on either side of the center. The tackles line up outside of the guards. Depending on the play, the tight end usually lines up alongside either the right or left tackle. Sometimes, the tight end will line up slightly behind the other linemen.

Unlike other members of the offensive line, the tight end is an "eligible receiver." This means that the tight end is allowed to catch passes. In most NFL offenses, tight ends are used to catch short passes in the middle of the field. Tight ends are also used to block defensive players, protecting the quarterback and opening holes in the defensive line for running backs. Because of this, tight ends are usually larger than other receivers. Some tight ends weigh 250 to 300 pounds.

Players like Tony Gonzalez, who are both large and fast, can be hard for defenses to stop once they catch the ball. Tony is faster than most of the linebackers trying to cover him, and stronger than most of the cornerbacks and safeties that try to stop him from running with the ball.

(Go back to page 19.) ◀◀

The Boys and Girls Clubs of America

One of the charitable organizations that Tony Gonzalez supports is the Boys and Girls Clubs of America. This group provides after-school activities for children. The goal of the Boys and Girls Clubs is to provide a safe place where young people can hang out, learn, and play. There are 4,300 Boys and Girls Clubs nationwide—they can be found in every U.S. state. The clubs provide programs for children every day of the week. The Boys and Girls Clubs of America have welcomed over 4.8 million children into their programs.

Many of the young people who participate in Boys and Girls Clubs programs go on to very distinguished careers. Athletes such as Michael Jordan and Shaquille O'Neal, entertainers like Jennifer Lopez and Denzel Washington, and public servants like former NATO commander General Wesley Clark, each attended local Boys and Girls Clubs when they were growing up. All are now members of the Boys and Girls Clubs of America National Alumni Hall of Fame.

Tony Gonzalez works with the organization both in the Kansas City area and on a national level. He has helped the Boys and Girls Clubs develop youth football programs around Kansas City, and donates tickets to Chiefs games to the group. He also visits local clubs to meet young people. Because of his dedication, in 2000 the Boys and Girls Clubs of Greater Kansas City named Tony Role Model of the Year. In 2006, Tony was inducted into the Boys and Girls Clubs of America National Alumni Hall of Fame.

The Boys and Girls Clubs are very active in the Kansas City community. Each year the organization serves around 10,000 children, ranging in age from five to 18. The clubs offer classes in photography, dancing, writing, and many other arts-based programs. They also provide athletic programs, such as Reviving Baseball in the Inner City (RBI), Junior NBA, and Junior WNBA. The Boys and Girls Clubs provide academic help with reading and computers. One of the group's programs is Power Hour, a class that teaches students how to do research and learn on their own. The mission of the Boys and Girls Clubs of Greater Kansas City is to promote "the development of self-esteem, values, and skills for boys and girls . . . with special emphasis on youth from disadvantaged circumstances."

Actor Denzel Washington (center) has served as a spokesperson for the Boys and Girls Clubs of America since 1993. Like Tony Gonzalez, Washington is a member of the club's Hall of Fame.

(Go back to page 22.)

Catch and Connect

When Tony Gonzalez commits to something—whether it is running a pass route or blocking on the football field, or making an appearance at a charity event—he gives 100 percent. This determination has led to Tony's involvement in many activities that are not related to football. One such project involved Tony working with sportswriter Greg Brown to describe his childhood experiences with bullying in a book titled *Tony Gonzalez: Catch and Connect*.

Catch and Connect is a book about Tony's personal life. He discusses his success in the National Football League, but also describes his childhood. Tony tells stories about his youth, and links them to things that he feels are important today. Tony's book is written in an encouraging way. He wanted young readers to recognize that, no matter what their personal circumstances, success is possible. His message to young readers is that everyone faces adversity, and that people must face their problems and fears in order to conquer them. On the cover of the book, Tony wrote:

❝My story will give you a glimpse below my skin. You'll see I've faced the same challenges and setbacks many kids experience. I wasn't always a tough guy. In fact, there was a time when playing football frightened me. I've written this book to share with you the true stories of my life and perhaps change perceptions.**❞**

One of the stories that Tony told in the book was about the bullying he suffered when he was in middle school. Because Tony was afraid, and ran home or hid when the older teens showed up looking for him, the bullying continued. Tony spent his entire eighth-grade year looking over his shoulder. It was not until he decided to stop running and stand up to the bullies that the problem ended.

Tony Gonzalez: Catch and Connect was published in 2004 by Positively for Kids. In September 2005, Tony explained to *Sports Illustrated* why he had wanted the book to be written:

❝I wanted to get my story out for kids who are going through stuff I went through, like being bullied or being on welfare or being in a single-parent home. I wanted to say, 'You might be going through hard times, but I've been there and look where I'm at now.'**❞**

(Go back to page 28.) ◀◀

A Good Guy

Every year *The Sporting News*, a national sports publication, awards 99 athletes the distinction of "Good Guy." The award is based not on what the athlete does on the field, but on how much that person gives back to their community through charitable work. A player can have a horrible season, but still receive recognition as a "Good Guy." *The Sporting News* chooses athletes from all of the sports that the magazine covers, including professional football, baseball, basketball, and hockey; NASCAR racing; and college football and basketball. Teams nominate players for the "Good Guy" distinction, and editors at the *Sporting News* make the final decisions.

The Sporting News has named Tony Gonzalez a "Good Guy" numerous times during his career. In 2004, the publication named Tony the National Football League's number-one Good Guy. The magazine's editors praised Tony for all of his charitable work. They specifically noted his work with Shadow Buddies, the Boys and Girls Clubs of America, Shop with a Jock, and other programs.

(Go back to page 32.)

The Sporting News has named Tony a "Good Guy" numerous times for his charitable work. Tony has been praised for his support of the Shadow Buddies program and the Boys and Girls Clubs of America.

A Loss for the Chiefs

On December 13, 2006, Lamar Hunt—the owner of the Kansas City Chiefs—passed away. He was 74. Hunt had battled cancer for 10 years before succumbing to the disease.

Hunt had a huge influence on professional football. In 1960, he started the American Football League (AFL), intending it to compete with the more established NFL. At first the AFL was considered inferior, but by the late 1960s its best teams were as good as any in the National Football League.

The two leagues merged in 1970. The new league kept the name NFL, and the Chiefs and other AFL teams became part of the American Football Conference.

Hunt was a colorful and popular team owner. In fact, he is credited with coining the name "Super Bowl" for pro football's championship game. His Chiefs played in the first Super Bowl, losing to the Green Bay Packers, 35-10. In 1972, Hunt was elected to the Pro Football Hall of Fame.

One thing that Tony Gonzalez appreciated about his team's owner was that in the 1960s, Hunt had encouraged his coaches to sign African-American players. At the time, African Americans often experienced racism and discrimination. Hunt's direction forced other AFL and NFL teams to seek the best players, no matter what color their skin was. "Lamar said, 'I don't care who you are or what color you are, it's all about what you can do on the field." Tony said after hearing about Hunt's death: "Of all the different things he's done in his life, that was definitely one that was eye-opening."

In a show of respect for Hunt, the Chiefs added patches bearing the AFL logo to their uniform jerseys before the 2007 season. Clark Hunt, Lamar's son, was named the new chairman of the team.

(Go back to page 39.)

Vegan Lifestyle

After Tony Gonzalez's experience with Bell's Palsy in early 2007, he began looking for ways to improve his health. A chance conversation with a man aboard an airplane led Tony to read *The China Study*, a book that advocates a vegan lifestyle. Tony decided to try a vegan diet, one in which he avoided eating any animal products.

The Vegan Diet

Vegans do not eat meat, eggs, seafood, or dairy products. Instead, they eat many different types of fruits and vegetables, as well as nuts, beans, and whole grains. Such a diet has many health benefits. These foods are lower in fat and cholesterol than are animal products, so vegans have a reduced likelihood of suffering from problems like heart disease and cancer.

A Need for Protein

Very few professional athletes—in any sport—have adopted a vegan lifestyle. This is because sports place an incredible demand on an athlete's body. As a result, athletes need a great deal of protein in their diets. Protein helps to build muscles and repair damage caused by exercise. Meat and animal products are a major source of protein. In fact, professional football players typically eat large amounts of red meat. A vegan must get his protein from other sources.

For several weeks, Tony followed the vegan diet. He felt fine, until he walked into the weight room at the Chiefs' training camp. He was shocked to find that weights he previously had lifted easily now felt too heavy, and that he had lost 10 pounds. Tony considered quitting the diet. Instead, though, he sought help from Jon Hinds, a vegan and experienced sports **nutritionist**. Hinds taught Tony about some plant foods and supplements with higher protein. The addition of soy protein powder, flax seed, and organic oatmeal to his diet helped Tony regain his strength.

More Energy

Tony is not a strict vegan. He occasionally eats chicken or fish, although he avoids beef and pork. However, he takes his healthier lifestyle seriously. He did not find that the vegan diet affected his play. "I was like, 'OK, this is working,'" he told the *Wall Street Journal*. "I have so much more energy when I'm out there." Observers of Tony's career would have to agree. The 2007 season was one of Tony's most productive, and the 32-year-old tight end was named to the Pro Bowl for the ninth time.

(Go back to page 40.)

1976   Tony Gonzalez is born in Torrance, California, on February 27.

1993   In his senior football season at Huntington Beach High School, Tony is named an All-American.

1994   Tony shares Orange County High School Athlete of the Year honors with golfer Tiger Woods; Tony enters the University of California at Berkeley on a football scholarship.

1997   Helps the Golden Bears reach the Sweet 16 round of the NCAA Tournament; enters the NFL draft and is selected 13th overall by the Kansas City Chiefs; appears in 16 games for the Chiefs as a rookie, catching 33 passes.

1998   Catches 59 passes for 621 yards and two touchdowns.

1999   Emerges as one of the NFL's best tight ends, catching 76 passes for 849 yards and 11 touchdowns, and is selected for his first Pro Bowl.

2000   Catches 93 passes for 1,203 yards and nine touchdowns.

2001   On February 12, Tony's girlfriend, Lauren Sánchez, gives birth to their son, Nikko.

2003   Tony's 71 catches and 10 touchdowns help the Chiefs finish the regular season with a 13–3 record. However, the team loses in the playoffs to the Indianapolis Colts.

2004   Tony sets a record for most receptions by a tight end in a single season, with 102. His 1,258 receiving yards is the second-highest total by a tight end in NFL history.

2007   The Chiefs and Tony reach an agreement on a five year contract extension; Tony catches 99 passes for 1,172 yards and is named to the Pro Bowl for the ninth time.

2008   On May 27, Tony's domestic partner, October, gives birth to their daughter, Malia.

Accomplishments and Awards

NFL record, career touchdowns by a tight end
NFL record, career receptions by a tight end
NFL record, most receptions in a season by a tight end
Pro Bowl selection, 1999, 2000, 2001, 2002, 2003, 2004, 2005, 2006, 2007
All-Pro selection, 1999, 2000, 2001, 2002, 2003, 2004, 2006, 2007
The Sporting News NFL Good Guy Award, 2004
The Boys and Girls Club of Greater Kansas City, Role Model of the Year Award, 2000

Career Statistics

Year	Team	G	GS	Rec	Yds	Avg	Lng	TD
1997	KC	16	0	33	368	11.2	30	2
1998	KC	16	16	59	621	10.5	32	2
1999	KC	15	15	76	849	11.2	73T	11
2000	KC	16	16	93	1,203	12.9	39	9
2001	KC	16	16	73	917	12.6	36	6
2002	KC	16	16	63	773	12.3	42T	7
2003	KC	16	16	71	916	12.9	67	10
2004	KC	16	16	102	1,258	12.3	32	7
2005	KC	16	16	78	905	11.6	39	2
2006	KC	15	15	73	900	12.3	57	5
2007	KC	16	16	99	1,172	11.8	31	5
Total		174	158	820	9,882	12.1	73	66

G = Games
GS = Games Started
Rec = Receptions
Yds = Receiving yards
Avg = Average yards per catch
Lng = Longest catch (a T denotes a touchdown)
TD = touchdowns

Books and Periodicals

Albergotti, Reed. "The 247 lb. Vegan: Tony Gonzalez Is out to Answer a Question: Can a Football Player Live Entirely on Plants?" *The Wall Street Journal* 251, no. 20 (January 25, 2008), pp. W1–W4.

Althaus, Bill. *The Good, the Bad, and the Ugly: Kansas City Chiefs: Heart-Pounding, Jaw-Dropping, and Gut Wrenching Moments from Kansas City Chiefs History*. Chicago: Triumph Books, 2007.

Gonzalez, Tony, with Greg Brown. *Tony Gonzalez: Catch and Connect*. Kirkland, Wash.: Positively for Kids, 2004.

Montville, Leigh. "Chief Weapon: Kansas City's Athletic Tight End, Tony Gonzalez, Used Some of His Basketball Skills to Develop into One of the NFL's Premier Players at His Position," *Sports Illustrated* 9, no. 25 (December 27, 1999), p. 44.

Stallard, Mark. *Kansas City Chiefs Encyclopedia*. Champaign, Ill.: Sports Publishing, 2004.

Web Sites

http://tonygonzalez88.com

Tony Gonzalez's official Web site includes many articles about the star tight end, as well as career statistics, a photo gallery, and a link that allows people to send fan mail.

http://www.nfl.com

The official Web site of the National Football League.

http://www.nflrush.com

The NFL's Web site for young people contains games, contests, and video interviews with different players.

http://www.kcchiefs.com

The official Web site of the Kansas City Chiefs includes news about the team, summaries of games, video clips, statistics, and league standings.

http://tonygonzalezfoundation.shadowbuddies.org

The Web site of the Tony Gonzalez Foundation includes information about some of the star tight end's favorite charities.

Bell's palsy—a paralysis of the facial nerve, which results in an inability to control muscles on one side of the face.

complex—difficult to understand.

contract extension—an agreement between a team and a player who is under contract to play for that team that changes the terms of the original contract. The contract extension usually adds several years and additional money to the original deal.

defensive coordinator—the coach who is in charge of a football team's defense.

draft—in sports, the annual process by which teams select new players from the college or amateur ranks, with teams that performed poorly during the past season picking before those with better records.

Franchise player—in the National Football League, this is an official term that can be applied to a player who is eligible to become a free agent. By placing the "franchise tag" on the player, the team limits the player's ability to sign a contract with another team for a year.

Heimlich maneuver—an emergency method for treating choking. To perform the maneuver, the rescuer stands behind a choking person and puts his or her arms around the person. The rescuer makes a fist with one hand, and covers it with the other, over the choker's stomach. Then the rescuer presses his or her hands sharply into the stomach, pulling upward at the same time. This can help to expel food or a foreign object that is blocking the person's windpipe.

lackluster—lacking energy, excitement, enthusiasm, or passion.

nutritionist—someone who is an expert on food and its effect on health, and is trained to teach others about healthy eating habits.

philanthropy—a desire to improve a community through charitable activities, such as donating money or time.

scholarship—money awarded to a student to pay for school expenses. In exchange, the student may be expected to participate in a particular activity, such as one of the school's sports teams.

tight end—in football, a player on the offensive team who lines up at the end of the offensive line and is responsible for blocking opponents as well as catching short passes.

vegan diet—a diet that does not include meat or other animal products, such as milk or eggs. These foods are replaced in the vegan diet by fruits, vegetables, nuts, legumes, whole grains, and other foods derived from plants.

West Coast offense—in football, an offensive philosophy in which short passes to receivers, running backs, and tight ends are used to spread out opposing defenses and open scoring opportunities down the field.

page 5 "Very few players . . ." Quoted in "Gonzalez, Allen Named to the 2008 AFC Pro Bowl Squad," Kansas City Chiefs press release (December 18, 2007). http://www.kcchiefs.com/news/2007/12/18/gonzalez_allen_named_to_the_2008_afc_pro_bowl_squad/

page 7 "It means a lot . . ." Quoted in "Q&A with Tony Gonzalez," Kansas City Chiefs features (September 19, 2007). http://www.kcchiefs.com/news/2007/09/19/qa_with_tony_gonzalez__919/

page 9 "Tony saved my life. . ." "Chiefs' Gonzalez Saves Man from Choking to Death in Restaurant," SI.com (July 7, 2008). http://sportsillustrated.cnn.com/2008/football/nfl/07/07/chiefs.gonzalez.ap/index.html

page 11 "I was awful at football . . ." Leigh Montville, "Chief Weapon: Kansas City's Athletic Tight End, Tony Gonzalez, Used Some of His Basketball Skills to Develop into One of the NFL's Premier Players at His Position," *Sports Illustrated* 9, no. 25 (December 27, 1999), p. 44.

page 12 "It embarrassed me . . ." Amanda Cherrin, "Tony Gonzalez: Chiefs Tight End," *Sports Illustrated* 103, no. 11 (September 19, 2005), p. 32.

page 12 "The next year . . ." Montville, "Chief Weapon," p. 44.

page 19 "I'd never gotten a D-minus . . ." Montville, "Chief Weapon," p. 44.

page 22 "[W]hen you look back . . ." Khalil Garriott, "Tony Gonzalez: Chasing Greatness on and off the Field," Kansas City Chiefs features (March 10, 2008).

http://www.kcchiefs.com/news/2008/03/10/tony_gonzalez__chasing_greatness_on_and_off_the_field/

page 23 "The third year is . . ." Montville, "Chief Weapon," p. 44.

page 28 "The best part is . . ." Rick Dean, "Gonzalez Gets Long-Term Deal," *Topeka Capital-Journal* (September 14, 2002), p. C1.

page 32 "How about this image . . ." "The Good Guys NFL," *Sporting News* 228, no. 27 (July 5, 2004), p. 20.

page 35 "It's not about doing . . ." ." Cherrin, "Tony Gonzalez: Chiefs Tight End," p. 32.

page 37 "I've heard so much . . ." Judy Battista, "Sight Unseen, Gonzalez Gives Edwards Seal of Approval," *New York Times* (February 2, 2006), p. D3.

page 40 "Simplistically, we're very pleased . . ." Quoted in "Chiefs and Gonzalez Agree in Principle to a Five-Year Contract Extension," Kansas City Chiefs press release (January 12, 2007). http://www.kcchiefs.com/news/2007/01/12/chiefs_and_gonzalez_agree_in_principle_to_a_fiveyear_contract_extension/

page 41 "We're not signing any papers . . ." John Ryan, "Non-Wedded Bliss," *San Jose Mercury News* (June 29, 2007), p. B2.

page 43 "It wasn't the easiest [catch]. . . ." Quoted in "Gonzalez Leads Chiefs to Victory on Record-Breaking Day," Associated Press (October 14, 2007). http://www.nfl.com/gamecenter/recap;jsessionid=081762E2556A260B1BF239AB922B9143?game_id=29276&displayPage=tab_recap&season=2007&week=REG6

page 43 "He truly is the best . . ." Doug Tucker, "Fear of failure led to hard work for NFL's top tight end," *USA Today* (October 15, 2007). http://www.usatoday.com/sports/football/2007-10-15-2349564228_x.htm

page 45 "There are going to be . . ." Quoted in "Chief's Camp Buzz: Tony Gonzalez Talks Retirement," *Kansas City Star* (August 13, 2008), p. C1.

page 45 "If they crown me . . ." Garriott, "Tony Gonzalez: Chasing Greatness on and off the Field."

page 51 "the development of self-esteem . . ." Boys and Girls Clubs of Greater Kansas City, mission statement. http://www.bgc-gkc.org/main_sublinks.asp?id=4&sid=37

page 52 "My story will give . . ." Tony Gonzalez, *Tony Gonzalez: Catch and Connect* (Kirkland, Wash.: Positively for Kids, 2004), cover, front flap.

page 52 "I wanted to get my story . . ." Cherrin, "Tony Gonzalez: Chiefs Tight End," p. 32.

page 54 "Lamar said, 'I don't . . ." Quoted in "Lamar Hunt, Chiefs Owner and Sports Legend, Dies at 74," Associated Press (December 14, 2006). http://sports.espn.go.com/nfl/news/story?id=2697040

page 55 "I was like, 'OK . . ." Reed Albergotti, "The 247 lb. Vegan: Tony Gonzalez Is out to Answer a Question: Can a Football Player Live Entirely on Plants?" *The Wall Street Journal* 251, no. 20 (January 25, 2008), p. W1.

Numbers in **bold italics** refer to captions.

Amy Hunter lives in West Virginia with her husband and three children. She is a freelance writer and enjoys writing for younger readers. Amy is the author of *The History of Mexico*, another book for young adults.

PICTURE CREDITS

FOR WESTMINSTER
AND ALL GOOD DOGS

Grand Central Publishing
Hachette Book Group
237 Park Avenue
New York, NY 10017

www.HachetteBookGroup.com

Printed in China

First Edition: June 2011
10 9 8 7 6 5 4 3 2 1

Grand Central Publishing is a division of Hachette Book Group, Inc.
The Grand Central Publishing name and logo is a trademark of Hachette Book Group, Inc.

Library of Congress Control Number: 2010931128

ISBN 978-0-446-57591-1

The Bedtime Book for Dogs

BY BRUCE LITTLEFIELD
ILLUSTRATED BY PAUL S. HEATH

GC

GRAND CENTRAL
PUBLISHING

NEW YORK   BOSTON

COME.

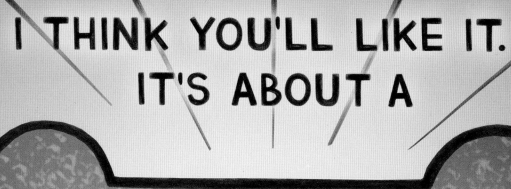

I THINK YOU'LL LIKE IT.
IT'S ABOUT A

TREAT

Once upon a time...

A VERY GOOD DOG WANTED TO GO PLAY.
BUT HIS FRIEND WAS BUSY.

HE FETCHED HIS LEASH.
(HE COULD CARRY IT HIMSELF.)

AND HE WENT OUT THE DOOR.
(HE COULD OPEN IT HIMSELF.)

THEN CROSSED THE STREET.

THE GOOD DOG WALKED TO THE PARK.

AND ROLLED IN THE GRASS.

BUT THERE WAS NO FRIEND
TO THROW IT.

THE GOOD DOG SPOTTED A SQUIRREL.

BUT THERE WAS NO FRIEND TO TELL.

THE GOOD DOG
DID HIS BUSINESS.

IT WAS NO FUN WITHOUT HIS FRIEND.)

HE RAN AS FAST AS HE COULD.